PUBLIC TOILET DESIGN

From Hotels, Bars, Restaurants, Civic
Buildings and Businesses Worldwide

Second Edition   Editor: Francesc Zamora Mola

FIREFLY BOOKS

A FIREFLY BOOK

Published by Firefly Books Ltd. 2013

First printing

Publisher Cataloging-in-Publication Data (U.S.)

A CIP record for this title is available from the Library of Congress

Library and Archives Canada Cataloguing in Publication

A CIP record for this title is available from Library and Archives Canada

Published in the United States by
Firefly Books (U.S.) Inc.
P.O. Box 1338, Ellicott Station
Buffalo, New York 14205

Published in Canada by
Firefly Books Ltd.
50 Staples Avenue, Unit 1
Richmond Hill, Ontario L4B 0A7

Printed in China

This title was developed by
LOFT Publications
Via Laietana, 32 4th fl. of. 92
08003 Barcelona, España

For Loft:
Editorial coordinator Claudia Martínez Alonso; **Editorial assistant** Ana Marques; **Art director** Mireia Casanovas Soley; **Layout** Cristina Simó Perales, Sara Abril Abajo

CONTENTS

INTRODUCTION

Bathrooms have traditionally been considered as an afterthought in the design of public places and areas. Public toilets are generally thought of as cold, and frequently non-hygienic spaces sometimes associated with delinquency and vandalism. Nevertheless, bathrooms not only form part of our everyday life but also reflect the evolution of hygienic practice, as well as express a range of human cultural practices to such an extent that they form part of the history of civilization.

In recent years, bathrooms have been subject to greater attention from designers, who give full rein to their creativity to turn bathrooms into an experience for the senses while also being imbued with great artistic value. This book presents a selection of very diverse projects in which bathrooms enjoy a special status as a vehicle for various artistic and cultural expressions, corporate values and the requirements of different social groups. Particular attention has been paid to the latter, as the needs of a male user are not the same as those of a woman, child, senior citizen or handicapped person — and the design of a bathroom must take these characteristics into account. Over the course of four chapters — Leisure and Culture, Hospitality, Working Environments and Community Spaces — we take in a survey of bathrooms belonging to different types of buildings, including bars, restaurants, theaters, gyms, offices, hospitals, kindergartens, public institutions, airports and train stations — all around the world — with special emphasis on the means used to bring together creativity and functionality.

It seems that designers are gradually rebelling against the long-standing conventions and status quo of bathroom design, and are creating spaces that are both functional and aesthetic.

Cristina del Valle Schuster

LEISURE AND CULTURE

Spectacular bathrooms can be found within bars, restaurants, clubs and theaters. Designers and architects no longer consider a bathroom a secondary space but, on the contrary, have started to discover the creative potential offered by this room and work their magic in areas of limited size. It is perhaps this latter factor that demands a concentration on functional solutions, while the element of spectacle implicit in these spaces makes entering them seem like an immersion into a world of fantasy and imagination.

ORHIDELIA

Architect: **ENOTA**
Photographer: **Miran Kambič**
Location: **Podčetrtek, Slovenia**

Orhidelia is a large wellness center designed
to connect with the natural surroundings. The
complex appears to be designed to merge with
the landscape with faceted elevations of reflecting
glass and a structure reminiscent of trees. The
organic, nature-inspired interior design relies
heavily on the balance between the indoors and
nature, creating a serene space.There is nothing
more relaxing than bathing while surrounded by
the beauty of nature. Colors are well balanced and
chosen for each specific space: bright and soft
for the areas visually connected with the exterior,
and dark and muted for the more interior rooms,
including the bathrooms.

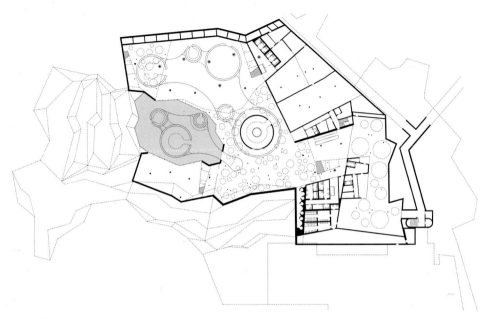

Ground floor plan

Second floor plan

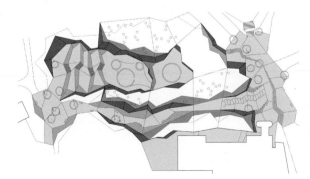

Roof plan

The design of the bathrooms is striking, but retains a relaxing feel thanks to the natural theme and subdued color scheme. Combined with warm shades of gray, the black plumbing fixtures make a dramatic and sophisticated statement.

YOGA DEVA

Architect: **Blank Studio**
Photographer: **Timmerman Photography**
Location: **Gilbert, AZ**

Yoga Deva is composed of a sequence of spaces
primarily designed to remove the visitor from the
exterior visual environment in every way. Visitors
enter through a long and narrow space dimly lit by
cove lighting; this produces a calming ambiance
that puts users of the studio in the right mood.
Aluminum leaf gilding and walnut veneer wall
finishes combine with the walnut millwork and
sparse decor. This contrasts with the main studio,
bathrooms, changing facilities and massage room,
which are flooded with light. There, the interplay of
light is calming and ever-changing.

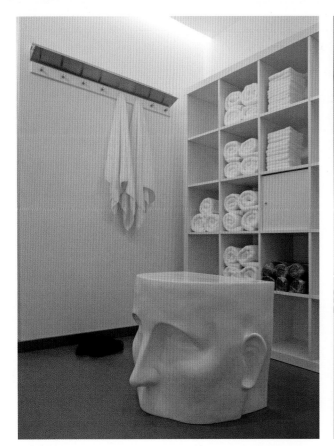

Floor plan

1. Entry
2. Yoga room
3. Changing area
4. Shower / Bathroom
5. Retail room

COCOON CLUB

Architect: **3deluxe**
Photographer: **Emanuel Raab**
Location: **Frankfurt, Germany**

Splashes of darkness swathe the interior of this bathroom in the form of anthracite-gray layers that cut across the walls and ceiling. This effect is complemented by the black terrazzo floor, the doors hidden behind a fractal image in cold colors setting off the texture of the pine branches, and the cloudy mirrors (with installed monitors) above each sink, an expression of the vital constants of all things without life.

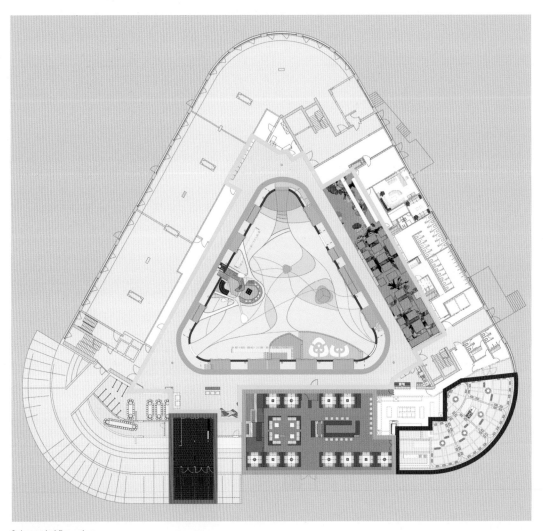

Color-coded floor plan

▨▨▨▨ Entrance: ca. 829 sq. ft. (77 m²)

▨▨▨▨ Micro ClubRestaurant: ca. 3,434 sq. ft. (319 m²)

▨▨▨▨ Silk BedRestaurant: ca. 2,239 sq. ft. (208 m²)

▨▨▨▨ InBetween with lounge: ca. 6,534 sq. ft. (607 m²)

▨▨▨▨ CocoonClub incl. membrane wall: ca. 8,514 sq. ft. (791 m²)

KARTEL

Architect: **Dariel Studio**
Photographer: **Derryck Menere**
Location: **Shanghai, China**

In the former Shanghai French Concession, Chinese- and European-style architecture forms a pleasant mix. This is the backdrop to Kartel, a three-story lounge bar occupying a refurbished existing building. The structure of the building, revealed during demolition, inspired the design of the lounge bar. Exposed concrete walls, stripped-down columns and art deco tile floors are incorporated into the design, contrasting with new elements. An example of this is the elaborate toilet stall, which makes a clearly discernible supplement to the historical building.

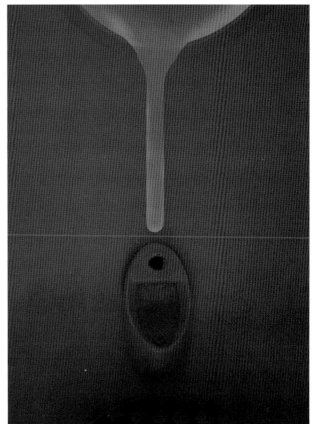

This toilet stall stands out due to its shape, material and visual impact without infringing on the integrity of the old structure. While making a strong design statement, the oval cylinder meets the needs of the building's new design.

CLUB MUSÉE

Architect: **Parolio & Euphoria Lab**
Photographer: **Maria Primo**
Location: **Madrid, Spain**

Parolio created the branding identity and interior design for Club Musée, blending art gallery and night club in a sharp, trendy way with a strong sense of drama. Photography, video installation, and illustrations by renowned artists combine with elegant black glass covering the walls of the club. Following a bold aesthetic inspired by Op and Pop Art, Parolio dresses up the bathrooms with electric pink for the ladies and magnetic blue for the gents, then adorns them with sensual line drawings signed with the club's slogan: "Art You!"

RGB and white LED backlighting provides enough light on the walls and floor without having to turn up the desired dim light level, which is an integral aspect of the club's design.

NISHA ACAPULCO BAR LOUNGE

Architect: **Pascal Arquitectos**
Photographer: **Sófocles Hernández**
Location: **Acapulco, Mexico**

Restrooms of the Nisha Club in Acapulco are treated as lounges. The women's area is red with a white bench and a palm tree at the center; the men's section is black and blue with a decorative triangular planter. The use of color and dramatic lighting in both lounges creates a unique visual experience complemented by the music, images, video installations and overall atmosphere.

KABARET'S PROPHECY

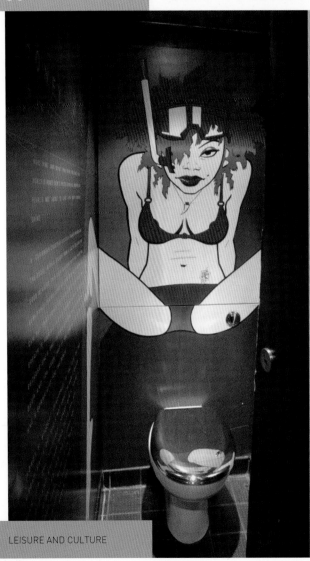

Architect: **David Collins**
Photographers: **Adrian Wilson, Tim Jenkins**
Location: **London, UK**

The bathrooms of the Kabaret's Prophecy club are conceived as places for socializing and therefore transcend the normal functionality of a toilet. Thanks to the work of the illustrator Jamie Hewlett, creator of *Tank Girl* and the visual image of the musical group Gorillaz, the bathrooms create an atmosphere that is both outlandish and intimate. They are adorned with Hewlett's drawings, which show insolent young men and ultra-sexy females in suggestive postures.

The daring texts dotting the walls of the bathroom are complemented by fragmented images of lips and legs, as well as young women oozing sensuality. Kabaret's Prophecy reasserts the importance of the bathroom as a design space, without which no bar or club would be complete.

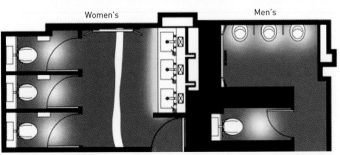

Women's   Men's

Section

LE BOUTIQUE CLUB

Architect: **Parolio & Euphoria Lab**
Photographer: **Juan Baraja**
Location: **Madrid, Spain**

The concept and interior design of Le Boutique Club celebrates the spirit of fashion and trendy showrooms with laser cut metal and wood, granite, leather, printed leather, glass, sculptural lamps and large backlit surfaces. The same level of detail is carried out in the bathrooms, with walls that are covered with photographic images. The mirrors are designed like fashion magazines, with clientele looking at their reflections as cover models.

PARIS

LONDON

BOUTIQUE HOMME

DRESS
TO KILL
GET THE
SUPERMODEL

THE
ULTIMATE
CARDIO
PLAN
LOOK &
FEEL GREAT

WHAT
SEXY
WOMEN
LOVE

100 BEST
NEW TECH
TOYS FOR MEN

30 PAGES
OF STYLE
OUR TOP TRENDS
OF THE SEASON

MAN OF
THE YEAR
YOU HAVE WHAT IT TAKES

45

The women's bathroom pays
homage to supermodels.
The stall doors are a wink to
catwalks and are hallmarked
with the names of legendary
models. Inside, mirrors and
lighting facilitate LED backlit
illustrations of famous models.

SPAZIO A4

Architect: **Simone Micheli**
Photographer: **Maurizio Marcato**
Location: **Piemonte, Italy**

This club was designed as a large, multipurpose space that attempts to break free of stereotypes by creating a new relationship between the setting and the clientele. The bathrooms, which are accessed through a curtain that replaces the conventional door, are preceded by an anteroom complete with 13 computer screens that seem to observe the visitor's moves.

In these bathrooms black is the main color, interrupted only by the bright red on the mirrors and the cubicle doors.

CASA COR 2003

Architect: **Marcelo Sodré**
Photographer: **Tuca Reines**
Location: **São Paulo, Brazil**

The mirrors above the sinks are no ordinary
reflective surfaces but LCD screens that project
images of the bathroom's users taken by hidden
cameras. The effect is strange and slightly
disturbing, although it helps contribute to an
overall feeling of calm and luminosity.

CAMPUS CENTER IN ILLINOIS

Architect: **OMA**
Photographer: **Philippe Ruault**
Location: **Chicago, IL**

This building on the campus of the Illinois Institute of Technology was designed to organize the dense network of pathways connecting the different parts of the campus. The bathrooms were drawn up on the basis of a triangle, with the urinals and the sinks spread along two sides and the central space left open to facilitate circulation.

DAYCARE IN PAMPLONA

Architect: **Capilla Vallejo Arquitectos**
Photographer: **José Manuel Cutillas**
Location: **Pamplona, Spain**

Architecture is clear, elemental and perfect when it expresses a culture's values. The carefully thought out design of this daycare perhaps reflects Giuseppe Terragni's intention when he built a playschool in Como. The bathroom has been drawn up as an unpretentious space that is flooded with light.

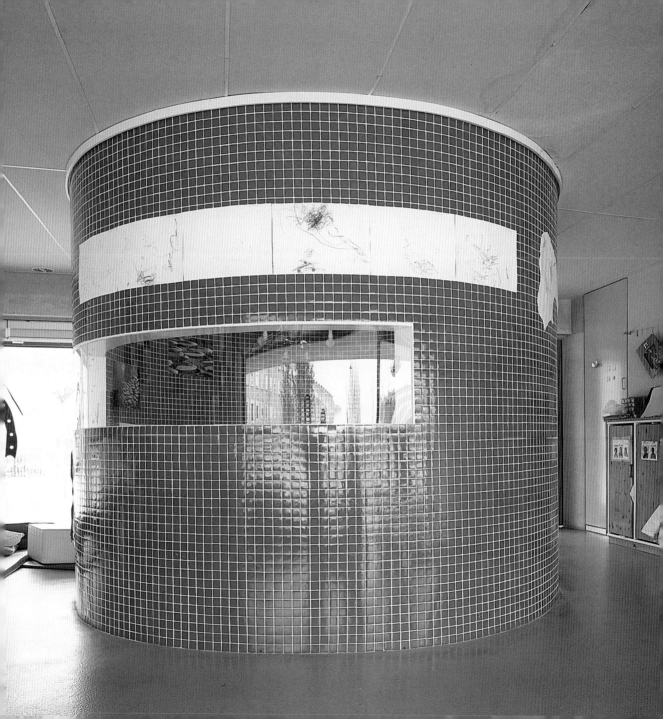

CINECITY TRIESTE MULTIPLEX

Architect: **Andrea Viviani**
Photographer: **Alberto Ferrero**
Location: **Trieste, Italy**

Who says that unique public toilets can only be found in bars and clubs? This bathroom, found in a multiscreen movie theater complex, gives particular prominence to color and graphic design, creating a distinctive, youthful setting. Ingenious and amusing pictograms show the way through an acid-green tunnel that leads to bathrooms assigned to ladies, gents and disabled people.

The typeface and pictograms
used in the bathrooms convey
a fresh, modern image that
corresponds with the young
clientele they were designed for.

CENTRAL LIBRARY ROTTERDAM

Architect: **Architectenbureau Van den Broek en Bakema**
Photographer: **Arjen Veldt Photography**
Location: **Rotterdam, the Netherlands**

The refurbishment of this library in Rotterdam incorporates new bathrooms designed as free elements in space, surrounded by the light that shines through the glass walls, where letters forming the Dutch word for "bathroom" are repeated. One bathroom is reserved for younger users, as you can see from the height of the toilets, each painted with a background of playful colors.

Fr. *toilette*, verkleiningsvorm van *toile*(linnen,doek)) 1 (-ten) (veroud.) kaptafel 2 (g.

heeft of waarin hij of zij zich bij een bep. gelegenheid vertoont: *zij besteden veel g*

toiletten, vgl. avondtoilet, baltoilet 5 (-ten) we (al of niet met wasgelegenheid

men bij het maken van zijn toilet no heeft. **toiletblok** (het) 1 (op campings e.d.

(m.); g.mv.) het gaan naar het toil 5). **toiletgarnituur** (het), st toiletbenodig

juffrouw die toezicht houdt in een toilet in een openba gelegenheid en zorgt voor zeep, handdoeke

toiletpapier (het), closetpapier. toiletpoeder (het), de (m.) poeder. **toiletpot** (de (m.)), de pot van het

r men toilet maakt, syn. spiegel, **toiletspons** (de), fijne spons die men g

aren en vervoeren van

aben kloeen. (ook wederk.) *zich

etsp* **toiletzak** (de (m.))

The interior of each of the stalls making up the bathroom space resembles Parcheesi chips, creating a relaxed, cheerful setting.

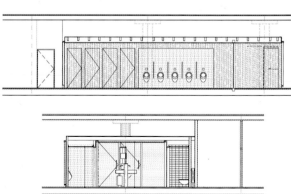

Section

NISHA MEXICO CITY BAR LOUNGE

Architect: **Pascal Arquitectos**
Photographers: **Sófocles Hernández and Jaime Navarro**
Location: **Mexico City, Mexico**

The design of the Nisha Bar Lounge in Mexico City is faithful to the aesthetics of the franchise. The men's and women's restrooms are two separate large gathering spaces with large windows overlooking a garden. Each has a service bar and a long sofa. The spaces are dark and sleek with accents of bright color provided by LED light walls.

MARK TAPER FORUM RENOVATION

Architect: **Rios Clementi Hale Studios**
Photographers: **Tom Bonner, Craig Schwartz**
Location: **Los Angeles, CA**

The Mark Taper Forum's auditorium was subject to an extensive remodel of its lobbies, backstage areas and theatrical systems. The updated spaces pay homage to the beautiful form and geometry of the 1967 Welton Becket-designed building. Part of the remodel focused on providing patrons with larger and improved restroom facilities. The circular flow of the restrooms directs patrons into the facilities, providing immediate access to the stalls, which cater to twice as many guests as before the remodel.

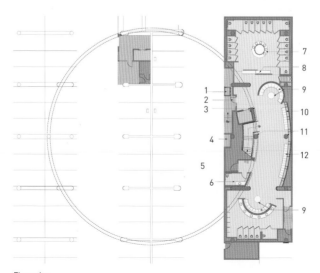

Floor plan

1. Wheelchair elevator
2. VIP entry
3. Curtain
4. Elevator equipment
5. Drive aisle
6. Family restroom
7. Island sinks
8. Vanity mirrors
9. Sofa and settee
10. Backlit glass wall with display
11. Mirrored columns
12. Seating

A 12-foot (3.7 m) diameter marble hand-washing station and vanity counter distinguish the extra spacious ladies' room. Above the circular structure, rotating mirrors are attached to stainless steel bars extending to the ceiling.

MAN TONG KITCHEN

Architect: **B.Y. Architects and Point of View**
Photographer: **Albert Comper**
Location: **Melbourne, Australia**

Designed by B.Y. Architects, the Man Tong Kitchen interior follows a contemporary ideal of traditional Chinese style, with a very rich combination of materials and vibrant colors. POV was responsible for the lighting design, bestowing the different spaces with adequate ambient light. The resulting lighting scheme fulfills a taste for ambient light with strong accents, drama and intimacy. The lighting plays with the dimmed aesthetic and increases contrasts, emphasizing red, gold and green to let these tones dominate the space.

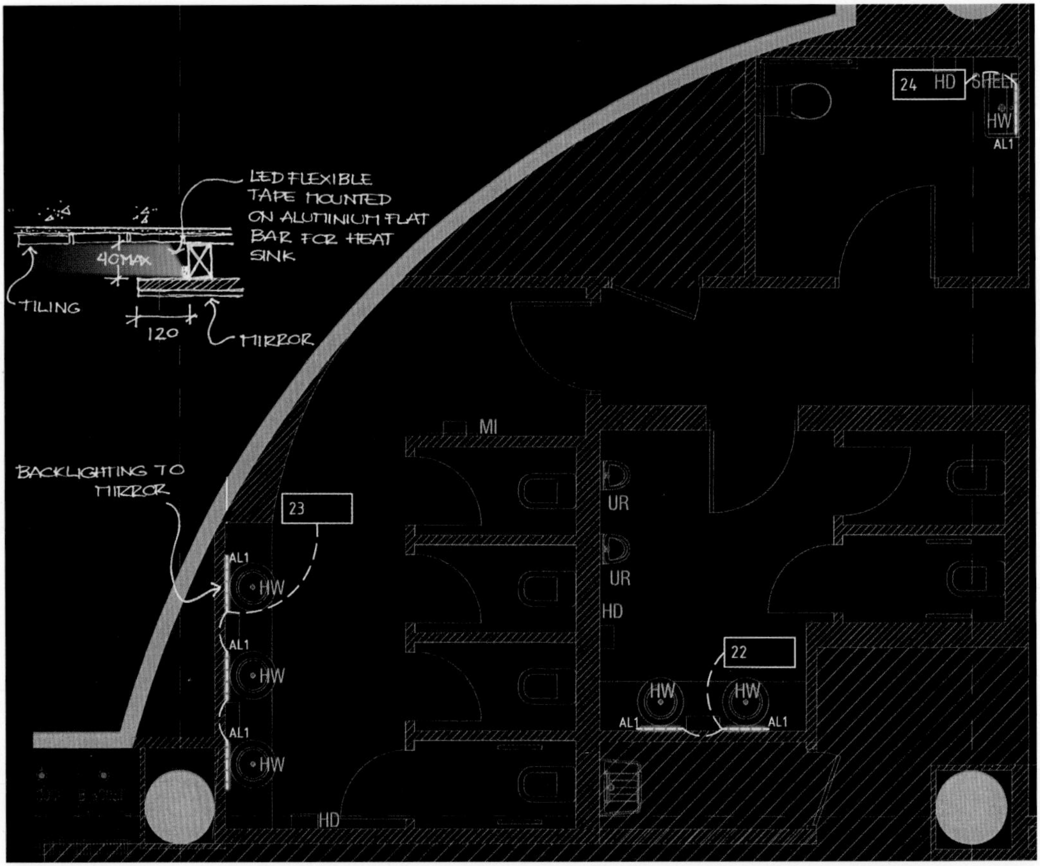

LED FLEXIBLE TAPE MOUNTED ON ALUMINIUM FLAT BAR FOR HEAT SINK
40 MAX
TILING
120
MIRROR
BACKLIGHTING TO MIRROR
24 HD
SHELF
HW
AL1
MI
UR
UR
HD
23
22
HW
HW
HW
HW
HW
AL1
AL1
AL1
AL1
AL1
HD

Lighting plan and details

The lighting in the restrooms effectively accentuates the richness of the materials and finishes used, and brings out the decorative elements.

L'OLIO COLTO

Architect: **mag.MA architetture**
Photographer: **Alberto Piovano**
Location: **Taggia, Italy**

The bathroom is reduced to an ensemble of planes that distinguish themselves by the different materials used in their surfaces. A horizontal band of iron sheeting, incorporating the mirror above the sinks, stands away from the wall and lets the light of a luminous strip radiate, adding visual depth to the space. The same material is used in the fabrication of all custom-made accessories such as the towel dispenser. The unit that supports the two sinks is composed of an iron structure and two wooden shelves. The welds and patina of the iron sheet are deliberately left exposed in reference to the handcrafted character of the items.

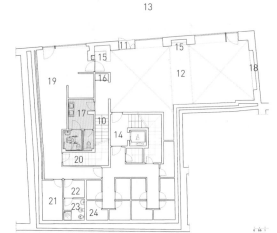

Ground floor plan (Bar and food shop)

Basement floor plan (Restaurant)

1. Portico
2. Entry from street
3. Bar and food shop
   - Hall
4. Bar
5. Office
6. Exhibitors
7. Closet
8. Internet point
9. Window stands
10. Access to restaurant
11. Entry to restaurant
    from courtyard
12. Restaurant - Hall
13. Courtyard
14. Access to restaurant
15. Office
16. Wardrobe
17. Toilets
18. Wine display
19. Kitchen
20. Closet
21. Storeroom
22. Dressing room
23. Bathroom
24. Cellar

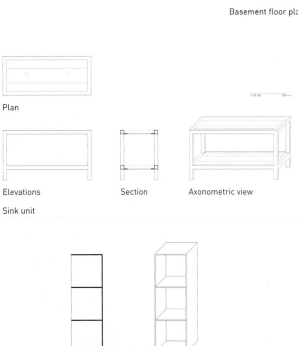

Plan

Elevations

Section

Axonometric view

Sink unit

Iron container for towels

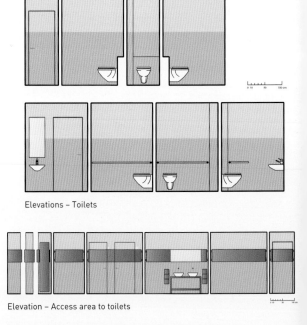

Elevations – Toilets

Elevation – Access area to toilets

MULTIPLEX CINECITY

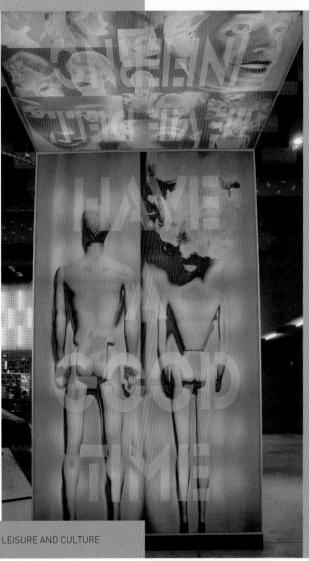

Architect: **Viviani Architetti**
Photographer: **Andrea Viviani**
Location: **Padova, Italy**

The world of advertising takes over the exterior
and interior of an existing warehouse located in an
industrial area. Bright colors, mirrors and neon
lights attract the attention of potential customers.
Once in the interior, the effect is intensified
and carried out, but not limited to the main
hall, popcorn counter, candy corner and public
bathrooms, as if intended to enchant and ensnare
the visitor. There are many references to toys
and arcade games. With this overpowering visual
display, the architect intends to trigger reactions
and emotions that only contemporary art with its
ambiguities and contradictions seems to be able to
provoke.

HOLLYWOOD BOWL RESTROOM RENOVATION

Architect: **Rios Clementi Hale Studios**
Photographer: **Jim Simmons**
Location: **Hollywood, CA**

Rios Clementi Hale Studios reconfigured walls, replaced partitions and added color and graphics to bring the restrooms at the Hollywood Bowl up to date and to improve circulation through the space. They installed lighting, glossy light-colored surfaces, white fixtures and mirrors to make the space inviting and reminiscent of the amphitheater's historic grounds. The green floor is suggestive of California holly growing around the bowl, and the black curvilinear graphics on the walls and ceiling are derived from an abstraction of the iconic concentric arches of bandshells.

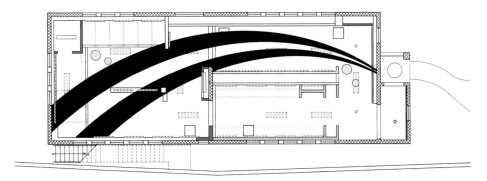

Men's restroom reflected ceiling plan

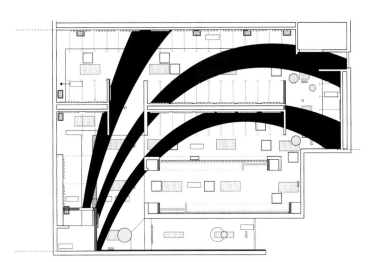

Women's restroom reflected ceiling plan

GRAVITECTURE M

Architect: **Shuhei Endo Archilect Institute**
Photographer: **Yoshiharu Matsumura**
Location: **Miki-city Hyogo pref., Japan**

The new ticket booth and toilet pavilion sit right next to a tennis court that had previously been built. The facility is contained within an oval ring made of bricks, which stands separately from the Corten steel roof and columns. The interior is as organic as the exterior, with partitions and fixtures conforming to the flows of the building shape. And while rectilinear elements are set against the curves of the building, their own design evokes the curvilinear theme through arches and rounded corners.

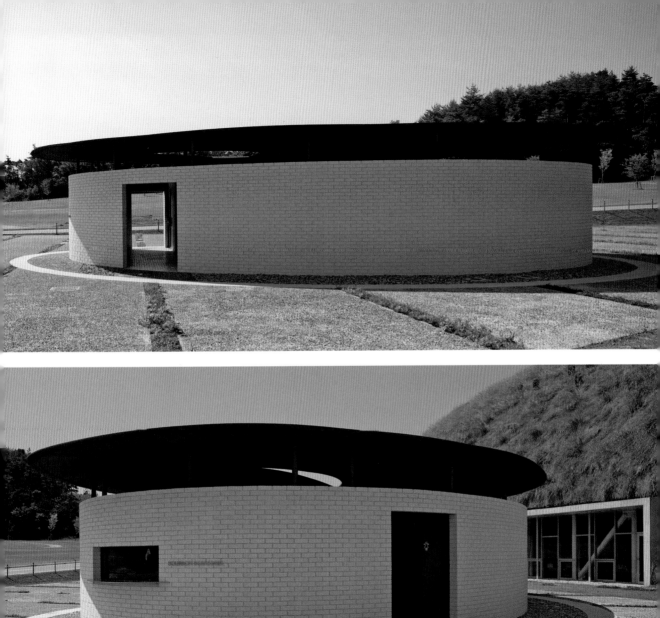

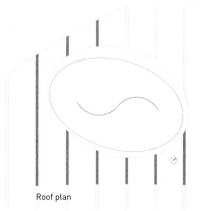

Roof plan

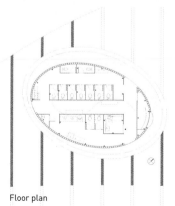

Floor plan

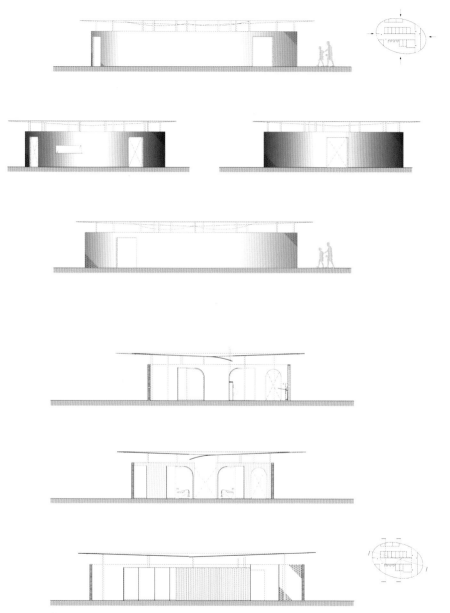

Elevations and sections

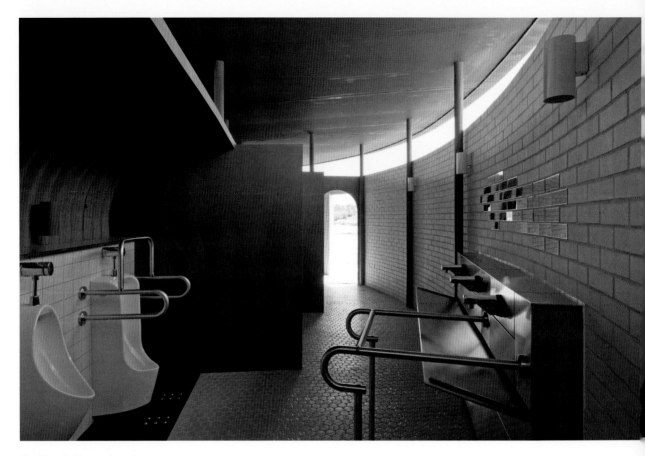

Far from being an obstacle
to a tasteful design, the
accessibility requirements are
integrated effortlessly into the
overall architecture.

TOKINOKURA LAVATORIES

Architect: **Shuichiro Yoshida Architects**
Photographer: **Sadamu Saito**
Location: **Chikusei City, Ibaraki pref., Japan**

Tokinokura Lavatories are contained in a tall narrow construction on less than 100 sq. ft. (9 m²) of ground floor space. Adjacent to a former stone storage building, which was turned into the headquarters of a volunteer group, the lavatories serve visitors and staff. In order to maintain the integrity of the existing building, the new structure is a freestanding building rather than an addition, and its simple design befits the history of the surrounding area. The structure, which houses a sink and two stalls, has plastered walls, a painted plywood ceiling with exposed laminated beams and a polished concrete floor.

The new building maintains
a preexisting stone wall as
a reference to the original
storage facility and displays
a combination of white and
transparent surfaces that
simply provide protection
against environmental hazards,
while also allowing abundant
natural light through a large
clerestory.

TROLLSTIGEN TOURIST ROUTE PROJECT

Architect: **Reiulf Ramstad Arkitekter**
Photographers: **Jiri Havrand, Jarle Wæhler, Helge Stikbakke and Per Kollstad (Statens vegvesen), Iver Otto Gjelstenli, Diephotodesigner.de, Wallpaper, Reiulf Ramstad Arkitekter**
Location: **Romsdalen, Norway**

The Trollstigen Tourist Route Project enhances the experience of the Trollstigen plateau's natural environment. Through the notion of water as a dynamic element — from snow, to running and then falling water — and rock as a static element, the project creates a series of relations that describe and magnify the uniqueness of the site. Poured-in-place concrete, glass and Corten steel are the materials chosen for a visitors' facility that includes a lookout, a restaurant and restrooms. These materials facilitate the maintenance in a location as remote as the Trollstigen plateau, with access roads closed during the winter.

Elevations

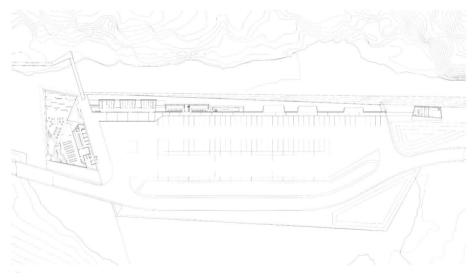

Floor plan

Water-saving vacuum toilets from Jets provide visitors with high sanitation standards. One of the benefits of this technology is the use of little water compared to traditional toilets, with more than adequate flushing capability.

SELVIKA, NATIONAL TOURIST ROUTE

Architect: **Reiulf Ramstad Arkitekter**
Photographer: **Reiulf Ramstad Arkitekter**
Location: **Havøysund, Finnmark, Norway**

This facility is a winding concrete structure in a barren landscape of breathtaking beauty. Since accessibility was a primary concern, the architects opted for a ramp as the entryway, which stands out as the driving force that defines the character of the design. The structure, which is self-sustainable in terms of power input and waste output, includes a picnic area with restrooms, a bicycle shed and a barbecue area. With two circular skylights that let in abundant natural light, the toilets are the only section of the structure that is not open to the landscape.

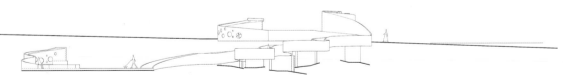

Northeast elevation

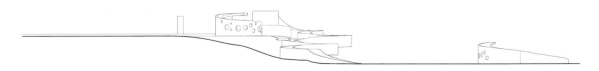

Southwest elevation

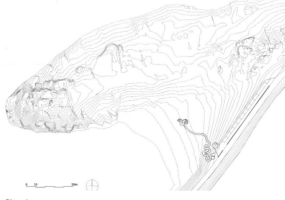

Site plan

The bathroom interior is minimal with stainless steel fixtures that adapt to the curvilinear form of the walls. Complete with high-end plumbing technology, the facility is self-sustainable in terms of power input and waste output.

HOSPITALITY

How do people choose which hotel to stay in? Besides location, price, amenities and service, guestrooms and the bathrooms in them are an important part of the decision. Bathrooms may be a separate room or an open extension of the guestroom. Hotel bathrooms can feature great interior design laboratories and have come a long way from being merely functional. Designers and hotel developers join forces to come up with creative ways to cater to essential needs and creating bathrooms that live up to guests' expectations.

HOTEL ALEPH

Architect: **Adam Tihany**
Photographer: **Alberto Ferrero**
Location: **Rome, Italy**

The public bathrooms in this hotel (entirely designed by Adam Tihany) are an intelligent continuation of the heaven/hell duality that echoes throughout the interior of the building. The totally red Aleph bathroom is dramatic. The effect was created by tiling the walls with red mosaics interspersed with strips of black Bisazza granite.

The bathrooms in the spa are very different in appearance from those in the hall. Pale colors and soft lighting are used to evoke the sky, creating a space that exudes relaxation and tranquillity.

GOLDEN TULIP ASHAR SUITES SHANGHAI CENTRAL

Architect: **Dariel Studio**
Photographer: **Derryck Menere**
Location: **Shanghai, China**

Golden Tulip Ashar Suites Shanghai Central is a fashionable business hotel in a refurbished 22-story existing apartment building. The different-sized apartments give room to spacious guestrooms more consistent in size with fully equipped facilities. Avoiding any traditionalism when it comes to decorating the rooms of a business hotel, Thomas Dariel introduces six different color schemes — pink, green, blue, purple, gray and black — using striped suit fabrics to cover the guestroom walls and marble and ceramic tile in the bathrooms.

Whether clad in tile or marble,
the design of the bathrooms
makes a strong statement,
using dramatic colors and
patterns, but is elegant so as
not to disregard the fact that
this is a business hotel.

HOTEL SIDE

Architect: **Matteo Thun**
Photographer: **c/o idpa**
Location: **Hamburg, Germany**

This project is part of the Hotel Side in Hamburg, created by Matteo Thun along with theater director Robert Wilson and architects Alsop and Stoermer. In the middle of an oasis in which sensory reactions are heightened by the lighting, and the space is reduced to the beauty of economy and simplicity, this public bathroom seems to have been borrowed from a stage set for an evocative and imaginative theater piece.

The lyricism of the lighting, softness of the colors and sinuousity of the concentric forms, which seem to embrace infinity, totality and timelessness, raise a setting often marked by tawdriness to a sphere of elegance and beauty.

RESTROOMS AT NEW HOTEL

Architects: **Fernando and Humberto Campana**
Photographer: **YES!HOTELS GROUP**
Location: **Athens, Greece**

The Campana brothers were commissioned to refurbish the Olympic Palace hotel in Athens for the Yes! Hotels chain. Stylish furniture and fixtures made out of salvaged items from the old building, and a thematic decoration inspired by traditional Greek themes adorn the striking interiors of the New Hotel. With the design of the bathrooms, the Campana brothers go beyond the basic functional needs, bestowing every fixture with a sculptural character. Separated from the bedroom by floor to ceiling jagged mirrors, the brass-finished sinks are molded to look like faceted rocks.

HILTON PATTAYA RESTROOMS

Architect: **Department of Architecture**
Photographer: **Wison Tungthunya**
Location: **Pattaya, Thailand**

Department of Architecture designed various
public areas of the Hilton Pattaya. The restroom
lobby is a transitional space, which while
functionally simple, still allows opportunities for
site-specific installations. The space is heavy
on ocean-themed details — most notably, the
ceiling in the main lobby covered in fabric sheets
is suggestive of rippling waves — with curvy lines,
warm lights, aqua colors, bleached wood and
sparkling mirrors. The use of texture and lighting
produce a theatrical atmosphere, enhanced by
large jellyfish-like chandeliers that radiate a soft
light across the mosaic-tiled walls and floor-to-
ceiling mirrors.

The atmosphere inside the restrooms is a stark contrast to that in the adjacent lobby. The lighting is dim, mainly focused over the vanity counters and sinks that are randomly arranged. Tall mirrors create a kaleidoscope effect, resulting in an unsettling atmosphere reinforced by a series of slanted wood slat screens.

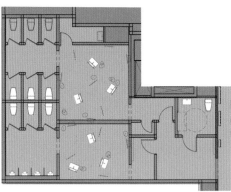

Restroom floor plans

BELVEDERE HOTEL GUESTROOM BATHROOMS

Architect: **Rockwell Group**
Photographer: **Rockwell Architecture**
Location: **Mykonos, Greece**

Belvedere Hotel is set in the context of the authentic traditional style of Mykonos' architecture. Inspired by the Aegean Sea, textural features such as hand-carved rosewood and white marble, sculptures by local artists, stunning views of the Aegean, and a color palette of whites, warm tans and greens are featured throughout each of the spaces. The predominant white shades, marble, hand-cut mosaics and monolithic sinks infuse the bathrooms with fresh beauty.

MALATESTA COUNTRYSIDE HOTEL

Architect: mgark | Michele Gambato
Photographer: **Michele Gambato**
Location: **Pergola, Marche, Italy**

The hotel emerges from the restoration of an existing farm composed of three buildings. Despite the limitations presented by the existing structures, the design incorporates clever details to create a relaxing haven. The interiors are completely redesigned to suit the needs of the hotel, and attention to detail was particularly paid to the windows. Their position, shape and size were planned to conform with the current building regulations and to open up the building to the exterior. The use of light reinforces the strong architectural features even in the simple bathrooms.

W PARIS-OPÉRA

Architect: **Rockwell Group Europe**
Photographer: **Rockwell Architecture**
Location: **Paris, France**

The 19th-century building across from the opera house was the object of an extensive remodel to accommodate the services of the W Paris-Opéra. The striking original Neo-classical interior is reinterpreted and infused with a contemporary and stylish flavor inspired by New York's energy. Every detail, whether it is in the restaurant or in the guestrooms is carefully considered; the same goes in the bathrooms, which display a practical design with trough-like sinks, double rain shower and freestanding bathtub.

The modern marble bathrooms don't seem out of place in the original Neo-classical interiors. Rather, the aesthetic mixes opulence with a relaxed style.

SALA PHUKET RESTROOMS

Architect: **Department of Architecture**
Photographer: **Wison Tungthunya**
Location: **Phuket, Thailand**

Sala Phuket Restaurant is designed as a pavilion with all its sides open to nature. In contrast, the service area is enclosed in a separate solid building with an interior courtyard. There, a random display of vanities serves as a surprising entrance to the restrooms. Shelter is provided by a series of canopies, which are a larger scale replica of the vanities. This unique architectural feature is a compelling mix of Asian accents and a neutral color palette dominated by white and grayish green tones. The Chinese-style bird cages and tall bulbous candlesticks provide the space with a strong theatrical appeal.

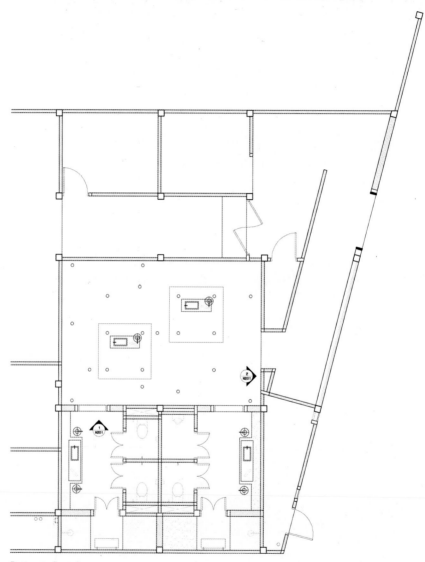

Restrooms floor plan

HILTON "CENTRO HISTÓRICO" HOTEL SPA AND FITNESS CENTER

Architect: **Pascal Arquitectos**
Photographer: **Sófocles Hernández**
Location: **Mexico City, Mexico**

Hilton "Centro Histórico" occupies the site where Hotel Prado, which was demolished after it suffered damages during the 1985 earthquake, stood for decades. In addition to the basic services, the new hotel offers a fitness center and spa, and a 3,000 sq. ft. (280 m²) garden overlooking Alameda Park — an attempt to immerse visitors in an atmosphere reminiscent of Mexico in the 1950s, when hotels were considered sociocultural gathering places. The hotel's atmosphere is achieved with spaces that benefit from exterior views and, more specifically, with the use of materials such as travertine, frosted glass and hardwood floors.

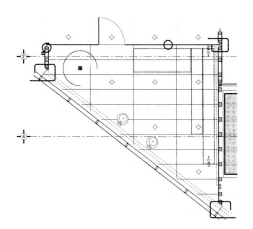

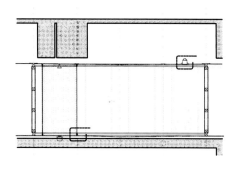

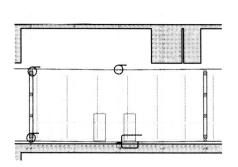

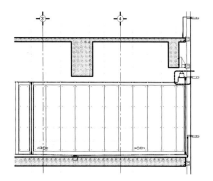

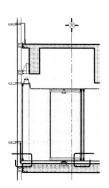

Men's sauna floor plan and sections

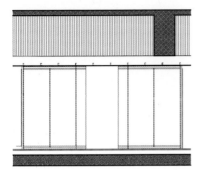
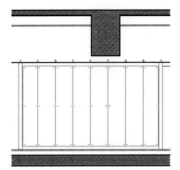

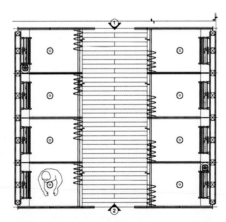

Men's shower room floor plan and interior elevations

WORKING ENVIRONMENTS

It is a proven fact that a well-structured bathroom fosters communication and improves the working environment, thereby also enhancing the performance of the labor force. At the same time, a bathroom can highlight a company's business values and provide information about its field of production. These factors are illustrated by the projects shown in this section — bathrooms in offices, stores, showrooms and shopping malls that present a functional and visually attractive design, especially adapted to the needs of the establishment, its workforce and clientele.

SOLENGO HEADQUARTERS' RESTROOMS

Architect: **Viviani Architetti**
Photographer: **Andrea Viviani**
Location: **Padova, Italy**

The interior design of this office space provides visitors and employees with visual stimulation by means of a combination of cool and warm colors, and glossy and matte surfaces that are enhanced by dramatic lighting. A series of backlit ink-jet printed X-ray images line hallways with black linoleum floors, while wallpaper-like tiles cover the restroom walls. It is in the restrooms where the architects seize the opportunity for a greater expression of color and texture, transforming a mere sink and vanity counter into an art object.

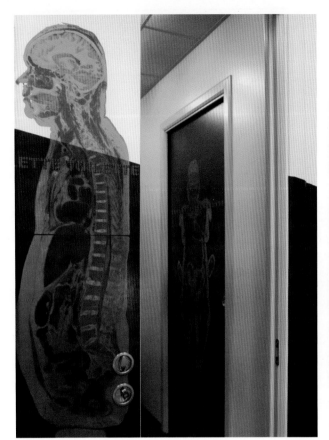

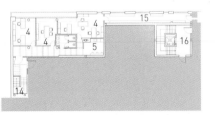

Lower floor plan

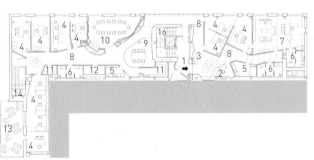

Upper floor plan

1. Entrance
2. Front desk
3. Waiting area
4. Office
5. Kitchen
6. Restrooms
7. Head office
8. Hallway
9. Meeting room
10. Main meeting room
11. Store
12. Server room
13. Terrace
14. Staff staircase
15. Archives
16. Main staircase

DURAVIT SPAIN

Architect: **Francesc Rifé**
Photographer: **Eugeni Pons**
Location: **Barcelona, Spain**

The design of the new logistical headquarters
and offices of the Duravit company used a green
material treated with resin to cover every surface.
The bright lighting provides overall illumination
to the minimalist space without focusing on any
auxiliary elements. Instead, these have been
picked out by indirect lighting from skylights that
point toward the walls.

OFFICES BISAZZA

Architects: **Carlo Dal Bianco, Mauro Braggion**
Photographer: **Alberto Ferrero**
Location: **Vicenza, Italy**

The architects designed an opulent, sumptuous bathroom with surfaces entirely covered with mosaics for the offices of Bisazza, the top-ranking producer of glass mosaics. The walls and ceiling alternate black pieces with fragments of white gold (24K strips in various sizes placed between two protective pieces of glass).

DUNMAI OFFICE

Architect: **Dariel Studio**
Photographer: **Derryck Menere**
Location: **Shanghai, China**

This project is an office space nested in an old motorcycle factory. The design reflects the company's dynamic nature and creativity and serves their professional needs. In this architectural approach the space was opened up to create brighter and wider rooms, and introduces playful elements such as the restrooms' entrances, which are designed to look like open elevator doors. Even the restroom walls are creatively designed by using images from video games to decorate tiled mosaics. The design illustrates that working in an office can be a joyful and unique experience.

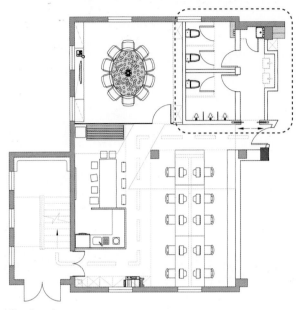

First floor plan

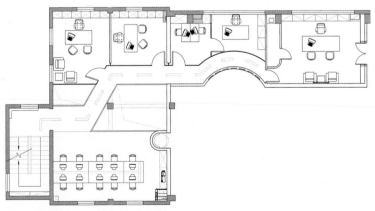

Second floor plan

Third floor plan

GEBERIT TRAINING CENTER

Architect: **Designrichtung**
Photographer: **Tom Bisig**
Location: **Jona, Switzerland**

The Designrichtung studio conceived the passage through the new training center for Geberit, the Swiss bath manufacturer, as a journey. The visitor goes down a cold, poorly lit hallway — an aesthetic aspect frequently associated with public restrooms — then moves through a curtain of water controlled by a remote control, finally reaching a second hallway inundated with colors and aromas.

The bathroom area is conceived as a high-tech space in which all the equipment operates automatically: the doors to the cubicles are activated by sensors, and the video sequences, projected on to the urinals, change as the user approaches the compartments, creating an artistic innovation that is in constant evolution.

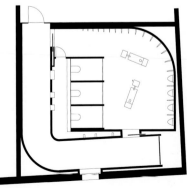

Floor plan

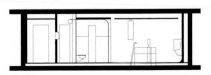

Section

NARDINI

Architect: **Massimiliano Fuksas**
Photographer: **Maurizio Marcato**
Location: **Bassano del Grappa, Italy**

The public bathrooms in this Italian distillery are set behind an entrance tiled with white mosaic. The interior has a light touch, thanks to the use of soft colors and glass surfaces, which contrast with the warmth of the Iroko wood flooring. The quality of the light and the delicate simplicity of the structure clash with the reinforced concrete featured in some elements of the interior.

BULLRING SHOPPING CENTER

Architect: **Amalgam**
Photographer: **Phillip Vile**
Location: **Birmingham, UK**

The bathrooms in this shopping mall contain cubicles that are separated by high partitions as well as private cubicles equipped with their own sinks, to ensure greater privacy. Indirect lighting systems are calming, while photographic images create a soothing effect through a series of different spaces adapted to the needs of various groups of users.

Areas specially designed for families include low toilet seats made for children, as well as folding chairs to provide greater comfort for breastfeeding mothers.

SIEMENS HEADQUARTERS

Architect: **Camenzind Evolution**
Photographer: **Peter Wurmli**
Location: **Zurich, Switzerland**

The bathrooms in the Siemens headquarters
in Switzerland reflect a concern to cater to the
needs of the company's workforce. A colorful,
modern-looking setting has been created to
transform the bathrooms into pleasant, cheerful
and positive spaces that transcend the usual
functional approach.

COMMUNITY SPACES

The following selection of bathrooms at sites like railroad stations and airports, or on the street itself, reveals a growing concern with vandalism and delinquency in these types of public facilities. Architects and designers go to great lengths to create safe, hygienic structures that are also visually attractive and inviting. Versatile materials and easy-to-clean surfaces are complemented by elegant, often minimalist exteriors that seek to blend into the urban landscape with the least possible impact.

PAVILION "DRAKENSTEIJN"

Architect: **BYTR Architects**
Photographer: **BYTR Architects**
Location: **Schiedam, the Netherlands**

The pavilion is positioned along a walkway between a playground and a petting zoo. In daytime, when the pavilion is open, two large pivoting walls create a welcoming gesture to the environment. At night, when the walls are closed, the volume is a luminous beacon. Two closed volumes are placed inside the semitransparent shell, containing bathrooms, storage space and a powerhouse. Sturdy vertical slats define the space without closing it off, blurring the boundary between the inside and the outside.

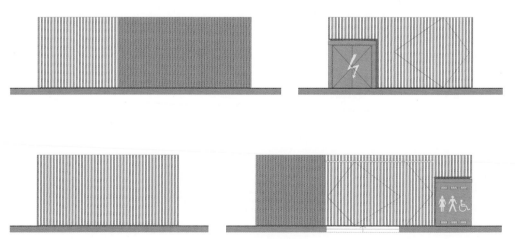

Elevations

The architects designed a vertical cladding with gaps in between. A colorful secondary skin is placed behind the vertical cladding, partially closing the elevation. This layered solution combines transparency and privacy.

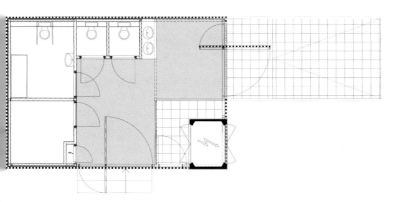

Floor plan

KUMUTOTO TOILETS

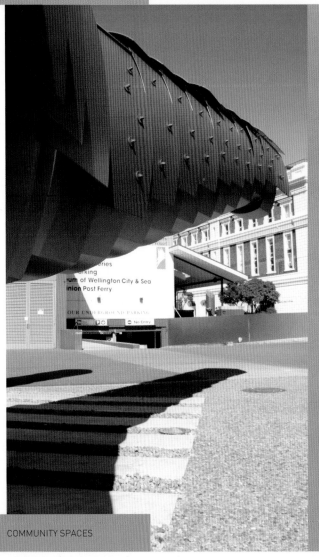

Architect: **Studio Pacific Architecture**
Photographers: **Studio Pacific Architecture,
Wellington, and Patrick Reynolds**
Location: **Wellington, New Zealand**

These highly visible and unusual public restrooms
integrate into the visual and historic context of
Wellington's waterfront with concrete construction
appropriate to the maritime environment and a
metal shell, painted the same brick red as the
neighboring sheds. Their design also takes into
account practical considerations such as security,
hygiene and vandalism. The eye-catching forms,
recognizable from all key pedestrian access points,
are suggestive of crustaceans or sea creatures.
Each form contains one accessible public stall,
with one of the two forms also including cleaning
facilities. The cantilevered "tails" of the shrimp-
like construction provides natural ventilation.

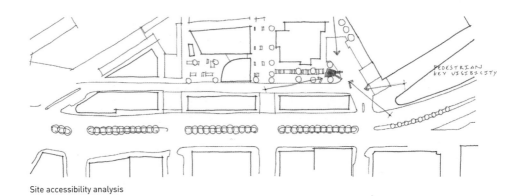

Site accessibility analysis

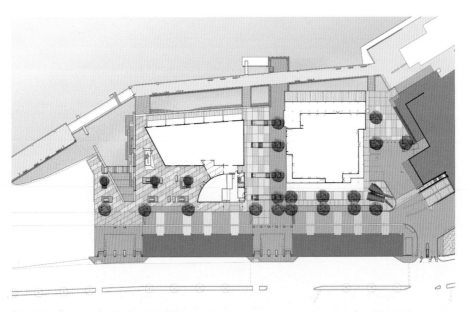

Site plan

North elevation

West elevation

South elevation

East elevation

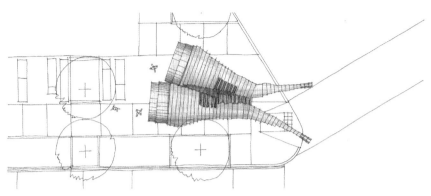

Top view of restrooms

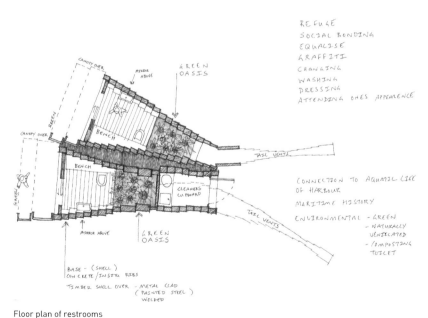

REFUGE
SOCIAL BONDING
EQUALISE
GRAFFITI
CHANGING
WASHING
DRESSING
ATTENDING ONES APPEARENCE

CONNECTION TO AQUATIC LIFE
OF HARBOUR

MARITIME HISTORY

ENVIRONMENTAL - GREEN
        - NATURALLY
          VENTILATED
        - COMPOSTING
          TOILET

GREEN OASIS

CANOPY OVER

MIRROR ABOVE

CANOPY OVER

SCREEN

BENCH

BENCH

CLEANERS CUPBOARD

TAIL VENTS

TAIL VENTS

MIRROR ABOVE

GREEN OASIS

BASE - (SHELL)
CONCRETE / INSITU RIBS

TIMBER SHELL OVER - METAL CLAD
        (PAINTED STEEL)
        WELDED

Floor plan of restrooms

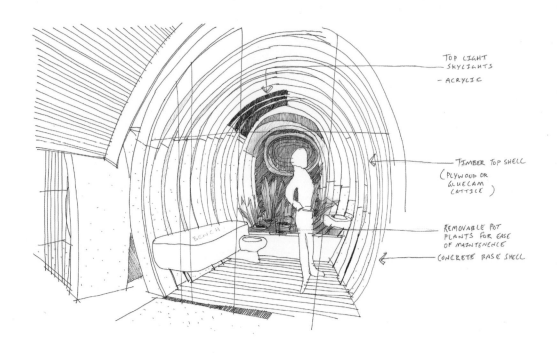

TOP LIGHT
SKYLIGHTS
- ACRYLIC

TIMBER TOP SHELL
(PLYWOOD OR
GLUELAM
LATTICE)

REMOVABLE POT
PLANTS FOR EASE
OF MAINTENENCE

CONCRETE BASE SHELL

BENCH

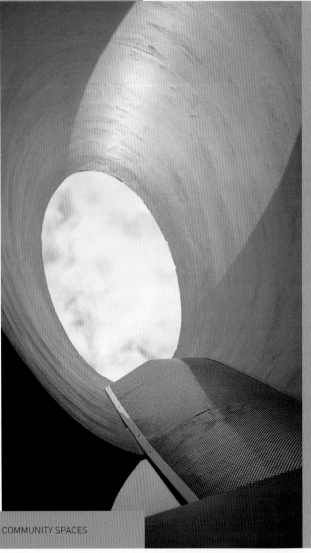

DIANA, PRINCESS OF WALES MEMORIAL PLAYGROUND

Architect: **Jestico + Whiles**
Photographer: **James Morris**
Location: **London, UK**

The design of the restrooms in this playground stirs the interest of children of all ages and backgrounds. Its bright colors and lively illustrations on the doors are inspired by Peter Pan, which is a recurring theme throughout the playground. A skylight situated above a double-sink module gives the space natural light and bestows a sense of expansiveness and luminosity to the project.

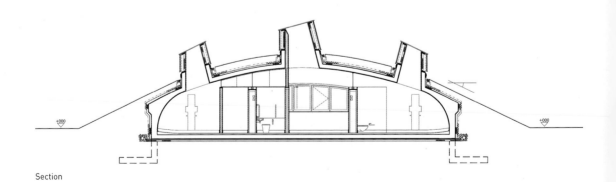

Section

A circular skylight endows this project with natural light, giving it luminosity and spaciousness that contrast with the sealed appearance of its exterior.

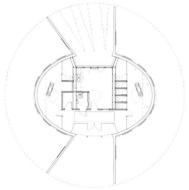

Floor plan

BRITOMART TRANSPORT CENTER

Architect: **Jasmax with Mario Madayag Architecture**
Photographer: **Elizabeth Goodall**
Location: **Auckland City, New Zealand**

The creation of a safe, visually attractive area was the primary objective of the refurbishment of this underground train station. This premise, along with the project's overall visual concept and identity, was also applied to the bathrooms. Consequently, resistant materials like stainless steel and concrete were combined with rich materials like mosaic, ceramics and glass.

In order to maintain high levels of safety and hygiene, sensory taps and soap dispensers were installed, along with self-cleaning toilets. The system of green and blue lights gives each cubicle a distinctive character.

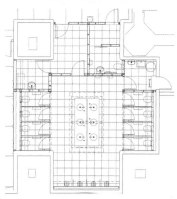

Men's restroom floor plan

PUBLIC TOILETS OF URQUIZA PARK

Architect: **Diego Jobell**
Photographer: **Luis Vignoli**
Location: **Rosario, Argentina**

The design of this public restroom is the second phase of a larger project that includes the renovation and expansion of a bar. The commission came with the challenge of having to create a facility that does not interfere with the daily activities of the park. The new facility makes the most of its location, generating an open space with easy access that includes a lookout and a playground in addition to the public restrooms. Materials were chosen to facilitate maintenance and for their relatively high vandal-resistant properties: reinforced concrete, polished concrete floors, Profilit glass wall system and galvanized steel.

1. Women's restroom
2. Men's restroom
3. Wheelchair accessible toilets
4. Storage
5. Lookout
6. Playground
7. Ramp
8. Staircase
9. Connection to bar

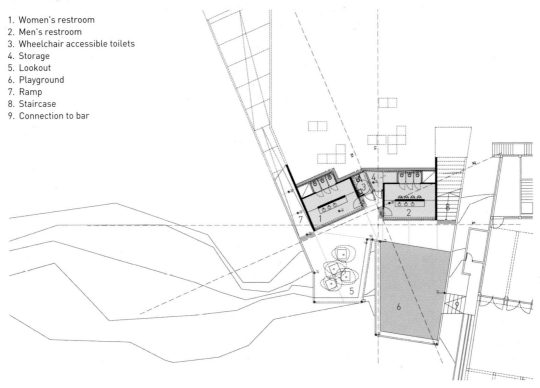

Floor plan

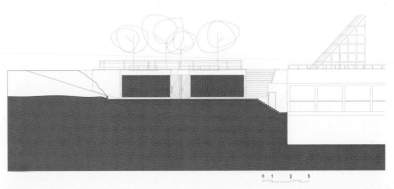

Front elevation

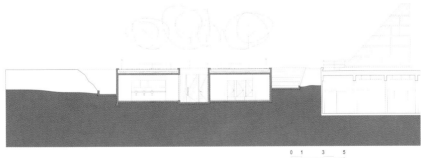

Longitudinal section

0 1 3 5

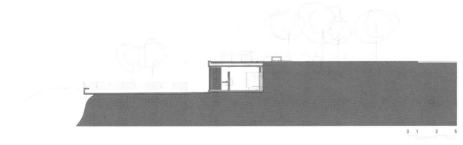

Cross-section

PUBLIC TOILETS IN SÃO PAULO

Architect: **Brunete Fraccaroli**
Photographer: **Tuca Reines**
Location: **São Paulo, Brazil**

Severity and informality present a harmonious
contrast in this showpiece of architecture and
design. The black Marquina marble highlights the
nakedness of the athletic bodies depicted on the
doors to the cubicles. These daring visuals are
not at odds with elegance, and the privacy of the
bathroom does not negate the uninhibited dynamic
nature of a stormy sea of waves.

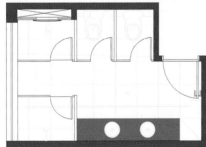

Floor plan

Section

SCHIPHOL AIRPORT AMSTERDAM

Architect: **Pilots Product Design**
Photographer: **Jop Timmers**
Location: **Amsterdam, the Netherlands**

First and last impressions are the ones that tend to stay in the mind, and this is demonstrated by the public bathrooms in Amsterdam airport, which reflect the nature of this country by means of the large images covering a range of surfaces. Tulips, windmills and sunflowers adorn what was once a stark, unappealing bathroom in an attempt to convert it into an unusual visual experience.

Opening the doors of this bathroom means stepping into a typically Dutch landscape, thanks to the array of images decorating the room, which set off an otherwise completely white space.

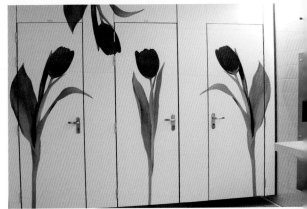

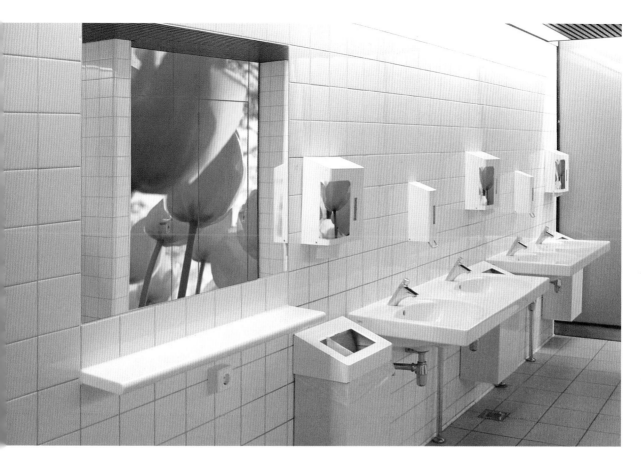

CENTENNIAL PARK AMENITIES

Female toilet

Architect: **Lahznimmo Architects**
Photographer: **Brett Boardman**
Location: **Sydney, Australia**

The brief for the project was to create a generic amenities building, which could be built throughout a parkland that borders the eastern suburbs of Sydney. The design strategy involved creating a linear landscape-driven building adhering to existing pathway systems or acting as a backdrop to the landscape beyond with minimal adaptation. The male and female restrooms were divided into two pavilions linked by a roof. The design incorporates sustainable methods of water conservation such as the collection of rainwater in a tank that is recycled into the flushing mechanism, and waterless urinals in the men's restrooms.

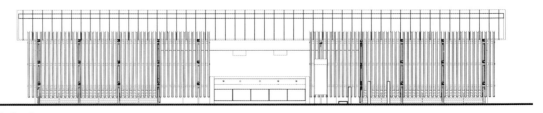

South elevation

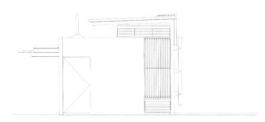

West elevation

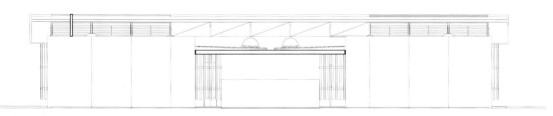

North elevation

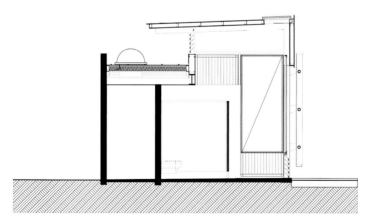

Section through typical cubicle + service room

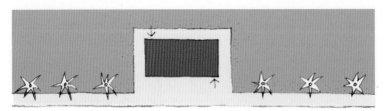

Existing amenities building: site analysis

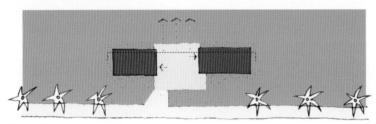

Proposed building: site analysis

Site analysis and entry

EXISTING CONDITIONS
Concrete "skirt" around amenities block
Building entries distributed around
    perimeter
Conflict in trying to attach an "object"
    building to a pathway system

SITE PRINCIPLES
Amenities buildings attached to pathwa
Consolidate entry points to minimize ha
    surface around buildings
Create landscape "frame," which would
    act as a "gateway" and allow visual
    permeability

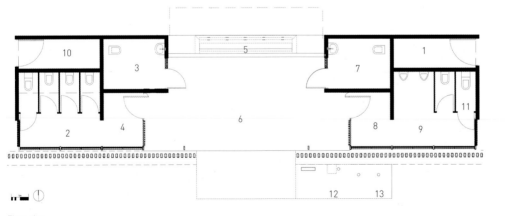

Floor plan

1. Service room 1
2. Women's restro
3. Accessible
    restroom 1
4. Women's entryw
5. Sinks
6. Breezeway
7. Accessible
    restroom 2
8. Men's entryway
9. Men's restroom
10. Service room 2
11. P.A.D. 2 cubicle
12. Dog bowl and po
13. Bikes

The space created between the pavilions fulfills the architects' desire to make the parkland part of the amenities block. The sinks are located in this central space, providing a unique experience for users, as they can wash their hands while looking out to the park.

PUBLIC RESTROOMS AT KADIKOY PARK

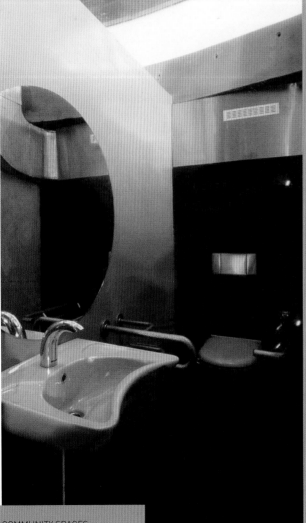

Architect: **GAD Architecture**
Photographer: **GAD Architecture**
Location: **Istanbul, Turkey**

The cities of Anatolia have a long tradition regarding sanitation services. This project was inspired by a desire to reassess the design of public restrooms and achieve a building that was visually attractive as well as safe and clean. For this reason, the interior used a range of cheap, resistant materials that are easy to maintain, such as concrete and stainless steel.

A narrow window in the roof
and the glass entrance doors
allow sunlight to enter this
underground bathroom.

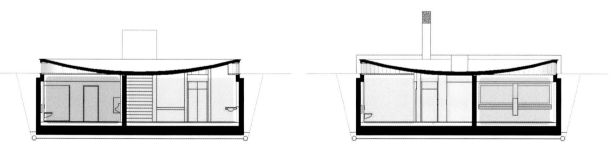

tions

DANFO URINAL

Architect: **Lacock Gullam/Oblique Workshops**
Photographer: **Speller Milner Design**
Location: **London, UK**

Drug abuse and vandalism in London made it
necessary to find safe, attractive alternatives
capable of accommodating the numbers of people
passing through the West End. The industrial
designers Lacock Gullam joined forces with
Swedish manufacturer Danfo to create this elegant,
metal urinal that remains closed throughout the
day and opens its walls after nightfall.

KROS URINAL

Architect: **Lacock Gullam/Oblique Workshops**
Photographer: **Speller Milner Design**
Location: **London, UK**

This urinal, permanently installed in the open air, seeks to curb urination in the street. The unit is only open at night — when the problem is most acute — and it stays closed during the day to prevent vandalism. The materials used can easily be cleaned and the elegant, essential design is intended to have minimal impact on the surrounding architecture.

DON'T MISS A SEC

Architect: **Monica Bonvicini**
Photographer: **c/o Galleria Emi Fontana, Milano**
Location: **Basel, Switzerland**

This revolutionary project by the artist Monica
Bonvicini was set up during the Art Basel 35 fair
to investigate the reactions of visitors in the act of
going to the bathroom. The module, comprising a
stainless-steel toilet and sink, was inserted in a
box of mirrors that reflect the outside world. The
occupants inside are surrounded by a glass casing
of startling transparency.

Inside, the occupant uses the bathroom while observing the world around him or her; from the outside, the module looks like an opaque, sealed box, which provides protection from curious onlookers.

PUBLIC TOILETS AT THE PORT OF DUBROVNIK

Architect: **Nenad Fabijanic**
Photographer: **Nenad Fabijanic**
Location: **Dubrovnik, Croatia**

In the old port of Dubrovnik, just behind the medieval walls, lies this narrow building measuring 5 x 41 ft. (1.5 x 13 m). The architect designed a structure with an elongated profile that would fit into this recently created passageway. Toilet stalls, doors and stainless-steel sinks situated in niches complete the ensemble, bounded by concrete exterior walls that contrast with the black stone inside.

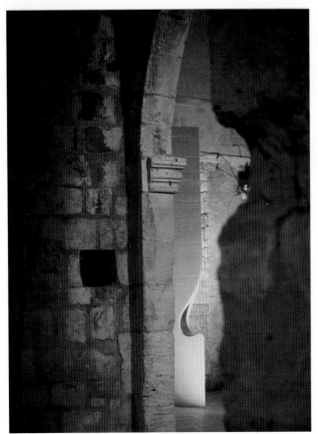

The interior, built with modern, industrial materials, contrasts with the city walls around this public bathroom.

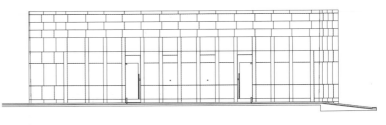

Floor plan

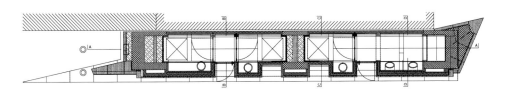
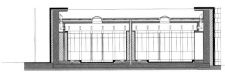

Sections

TRAIL RESTROOM

Architect: **Miró Rivera Architects**
Photographers: **Miró Rivera Architects, Paul Bardagjy, Paul Finkel | Piston Design**
Location: **Lady Bird Lake Hike and Bike Trail, Austin, TX**

The Lady Bird Lake Hike and Bike Trail is a linear park of scenic trails along the banks of the Colorado River in Austin. Forty-nine ¾-inch-thick plates comprise the restroom, which was conceived as a sculpture in the park. The plates are of varying width and height, ranging from 1 ft. wide by 1.5 ft high (30 x 45 cm) to 2 ft. wide by 13 ft. high (0.6 x 4 m) The plates are arranged along a coiling spine to form the restroom walls. They are arranged in a staggered fashion to control views and to allow for the penetration of light and fresh air. The restroom is wheelchair accessible and includes a drinking fountain, outside shower, urinal, sink and bench.

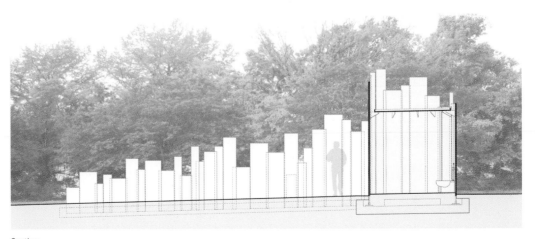

Section

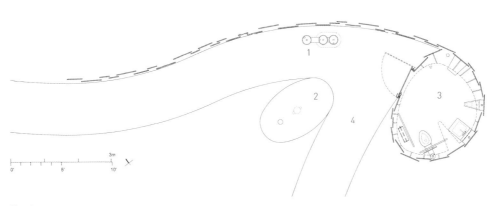

Site plan

1. Water fountain
2. Rise station
3. Bathroom
4. Path

3m
0'   5'   10'

ROADSIDE REST AREA AKKARVIKODDEN

Architect: **Manthey Kula Architects**
Photographer: **Manthey Kula Architects**
Location: **Lofoten, Norway**

The bathrooms at Akkarvikodden were built in connection with an existing rest stop and replaces an existing structure that had been lifted off its foundations by strong winds from the Atlantic Ocean. The restrooms are conceived to present a gentle break from the impressions of the surrounding landscape, offering an experience of different sensuous qualities. The structure of the small building is suggestive of the structure of a ship: welded steel plates locally reinforced with steel flanges — with every part specially designed for its specific use.

To prevent rust from staining the visitors' clothes, parts of the walls are screened with glass panels. In the smallest restroom, one glass panel is mounted in the ceiling. In this panel visitors can see the reflection of the horizon.

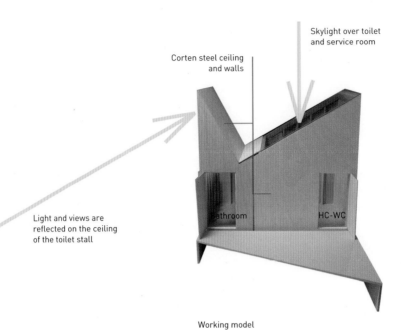

Skylight over toilet
and service room

Corten steel ceiling
and walls

Light and views are
reflected on the ceiling
of the toilet stall

Bathroom

HC-WC

Working model

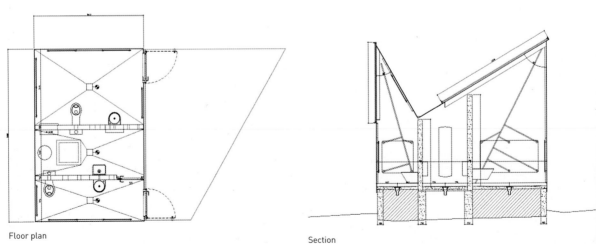

Floor plan

Section

DIRECTORY

3deluxe
Wiesbaden, Germany
www.3deluxe.de

Adam Tihany
New York, NY
www.tihanydesign.com

Amalgam
London, UK
www.amalgam.co.uk

Architectenbureau Van den Broek en Bakema
Rotterdam, the Netherlands
www.broekbakema.nl

B.Y. Architects
Victoria, Australia
www.byarchitects.com.au

blank studio, architect
Phoenix, AZ
www.blankspaces.net

Brunete Fraccaroli
São Paulo, Brazil
www.brunetefraccaroli.com.br

BYTR Architects
Rotterdam, the Netherlands
www.bytr.nl

Camenzind Evolution
Zurich, Switzerland
www.camenzindEvolution.com

Carlo dal Bianco
Vicenza, Italy
www.carlodalbianco.it

Capilla Vallejo Arquitectos
Pamplona, Spain
www.cvarquitectos.es

David Collins
London, UK
www.davidcollins.com

Dariel Studio
Shanghai, China
www.darielstudio.com/site/

Department of Architecture
Bangkok, Thailand
www.departmentofarchitecture.co.th

Designrichtung
Zurich, Switzerland
hindermann@designrichtung.ch

Diego Jobell, Architect
Rosario, Argentina
www.diegojobell.com

ENOTA
Ljubljana, Slovenia
www.enota.si

Fernando and Humberto Campana
São Paulo, Brazil
http://campanas.com.br

Jestico + Whiles
London, UK
www.jesticowhiles.co.uk

Lacock Gullam
London, UK
studio@lacockgullam.co.uk

Lahznimmo Architects
Sydney, Australia
http://lahznimmo.com

mag.MA architetture
Berlin, Germany
www.magmaarchitecture.com/home.html

Manthey Kula Architects
Oslo, Norway
www.mantheykula.no

Marcelo Sodré
São Paulo, Brazil
www.marcelosodre.com.br

assimiliano Fuksas
me, Italy
w.fu4sas.it

atteo Thun
an, Italy
w.matteothun.com

chele gambato architetto
dova, Italy
w.mgark.it

ró Rivera Architects
stin, TX
w.mirorivera.com

nica Bonvicini
an, Italy
if@micronet.it

nad Fabijanic
greb, Croatia
nad.fabijanic@arhitekt.hr

A
terdam, the Netherlands
OMA.nl

olio
drid, Spain
w.parolio.com

Pascal Arquitectos
Mexico City, Mexico
www.pascalarquitectos.com

Pilots Product Design
Amsterdam, the Netherlands
www.pilotsdesign.com

Point of View
Melbourne and Sydney, Australia
http://www.pov.com.au

Reiulf Ramstad Arkitekter
Oslo, Norway
www.reiulframstadarkitekter.no

Rios Clementi Hale Studios
Los Angeles, CA
http://www.rchstudios.com

Rockwell Group
New York, NY
www.rockwellgroup.com

Shuhei Endo Architect Institute
Osaka, Japan
www.paramodern.com

Shuichiro Yoshida Architects
Tokyo, Japan
http://homepage3.nifty.com/
shuichiroyoshida/

Simone Micheli
Florence, Italy
www.simonemicheli.com

Studio Pacific Architecture
Wellington, New Zealand
www.studiopacific.co.nz

Viviani Architetti
Padova, Italy
www.andreaviviani.it

INDEX